LEBRON JAMES

By Mike Kennedy

People We Should Know

Gareth Stevens
Publishing

Please visit our web site at **www.garethstevens.com.**
For a free color catalog describing our list of high-quality books,
call 1-800-542-2595 (USA) or 1-800-387-3178 (Canada). Our fax: 1-877-542-2596

Library of Congress Cataloging-in-Publication Data
Kennedy, Mike (Mike William), 1965–
    LeBron James / by Mike Kennedy.
      p. cm. — (People we should know)
    Includes bibliographical references and index.
    ISBN-10: 1-4339-0016-5 ISBN-13: 978-1-4339-0016-7 (lib. bdg.)
    ISBN-10: 1-4339-0161-7 ISBN-13: 978-1-4339-0161-4 (softcover)
    1. James, LeBron—Juvenile literature. 2. African American basketball players—
  Biography—Juvenile literature. 3. Basketball players—United States—Biography—
  Juvenile literature. I. Title.
  GV884.J36K46   2009
  796.323092—dc22 [B]   2008035567

This edition first published in 2009 by
Gareth Stevens Publishing
A Weekly Reader® Company
1 Reader's Digest Road
Pleasantville, NY 10570-7000 USA

Copyright © 2009 by Gareth Stevens, Inc.

Executive Managing Editor: Lisa M. Herrington
Senior Editor: Brian Fitzgerald
Associate Editor: Amanda Hudson
Creative Director: Lisa Donovan
Senior Designer: Keith Plechaty
Photo Researcher: Charlene Pinckney
Publisher: Keith Garton

Picture credits
Cover and title page: Brian Babineau/NBAE/Getty Images; p. 5: Ned Dishman/NBA/Getty
Images; p. 7: David Dow/NBA/Getty Images; p. 9: © Reuters/Corbis; p. 11: J.D. Pooley/AP
Images; p. 13: Courtesy Akron Beacon Journal; p. 14: Courtesy Akron Beacon Journal; p. 16:
Courtesy Akron Beacon Journal; p. 17: Tom Pidgeon/Getty Images; p. 19: Tony Dejale/AP
Images; p. 21: Jesse D. Garrabrant/NBA/Getty Images; p. 23: Mark Duncan/AP Images;
p. 25: Akron Beacon Journal/AP Images; p. 27: Jed Jacobsohn/Getty Image Sport; p. 28: Noah
Graham/NBA/Getty Images.

All rights reserved. No part of this book may be reproduced, stored in a retrieval system, or
transmitted in any form or by any means, electronic, mechanical, photocopying, recording, or
otherwise, without the prior written permission of the copyright holder. For permission, contact
permissions@gspub.com.

Printed in the United States of America

1 2 3 4 5 6 7 8 9 10 09 08

TABLE OF CONTENTS

Words in the glossary appear in **bold** type
the first time they are used in the text.

CHAPTER 1

King James

LeBron James was exhausted. He had given his all during Game 5 of the 2007 Eastern Conference Finals. Still, his team—the Cleveland Cavaliers—was losing. With less than four minutes left, they trailed the Detroit Pistons 88–81.

Game 5 was very important. After four tough games, the Cavs and Pistons were tied. The winner of the series would play for the championship of the **National Basketball Association (NBA)**.

The Detroit fans cheered. They thought their team was on its way to a win. It was time for LeBron to show why he was called "King James."

LeBron powers to the basket against the Detroit Pistons.

Royal Rally

LeBron drove to the basket and scored. After a teammate made a **free throw**, LeBron nailed a **three-pointer**. Then he threw down a powerful dunk that put the Cavs ahead. The Pistons responded with a three-pointer to make the score 91–89.

With 22 seconds left, LeBron rattled the rim with another dunk. The game went into **overtime** tied 91–91.

Crowning Achievement

LeBron continued his amazing performance in the extra period. When the buzzer sounded, the game was tied again, 100–100. LeBron opened the second overtime by hitting a jump shot. He made another and then stepped behind the three-point line for a long bomb. That tied the score at 107–107.

With time running out, the Cavaliers put the ball in LeBron's hands. He looked over the defense and darted toward the rim. Soaring past the Pistons, LeBron banked a shot off the backboard for the game-winning basket. He had scored his team's final 25 points! Two nights later, Cleveland won again and advanced to the NBA Finals.

Fast Fact

LeBron is not known only as King James. His other nicknames include "L-Train," "Video Game James," and "the Chosen One."

❝We threw everything we had at him. We just couldn't stop him.❞

–Chauncey Billups of the Detroit Pistons, after Game 5 of the 2007 Eastern Conference Finals

LeBron lifts the trophy for Cleveland's Eastern Conference championship.

His Majesty

LeBron has been unstoppable on the basketball court for most of his life. But his road to stardom was not easy.

LeBron grew up poor as the only child of a single mom. He had a speech problem when he was young and had trouble making friends. Once he found basketball, his life changed completely. Today, King James is a superstar on and off the court.

CHAPTER 2

Shooting Star

For some kids, playing sports is the perfect escape from a tough childhood. The basketball court, football field, and baseball diamond are the places where they feel safe and confident. LeBron James knows this as well as anyone.

LeBron was born on December 30, 1984, in Akron, Ohio. His mother, Gloria, was 16 at the time. LeBron never knew his father, and Gloria's mother died a short time after LeBron was born. Gloria had to raise her son on her own.

LeBron shares a laugh with his high school teammates. Playing basketball was a great way for LeBron to make friends.

Tough Times

Gloria had trouble finding a steady job. She and LeBron often had to move from one apartment to another. Money was tight, and they lived in neighborhoods where crime and drugs were problems. "We had some tough times," LeBron says. "But she was always there for me."

LeBron stuttered as a kid. At school, he felt that he didn't fit in. LeBron was smart, but he didn't always get good grades. When he played sports, he forgot about everything else.

Fast Fact

When LeBron was three years old, he received a toy basketball hoop. To this day, he says it's the best present he ever got.

Sports Talk

LeBron was stronger and faster than other kids his age. He was a star receiver on the football field. In basketball, he was a great all-around player.

A coach named Frankie Walker took an interest in LeBron. Walker knew that Gloria was having trouble making ends meet. He suggested that LeBron move in with his family. He wanted to give LeBron a stable home. Gloria agreed. Walker and his wife, Pam, had three kids of their own. They also had plenty of rules. LeBron did chores every day and had to hand in his schoolwork on time.

LeBron became best friends with Walker's son, Frankie Jr. Along with four friends, they formed a basketball team called the Northeast Ohio Shooting Stars.

Fast Fact

LeBron missed 87 days of school in his fourth-grade year. He had perfect attendance in fifth grade, after moving in with the Walkers.

> **"I had never coached a kid who picked things up and excelled in them as quickly as LeBron."**
>
> –Frankie Walker, LeBron's elementary school coach

LeBron's Mom

LeBron shares a special relationship with his mom, Gloria. She calls him "Bron Bron" and calls herself his biggest fan. Gloria usually sits **courtside** for LeBron's games. She is easy to spot. She often wears a jersey that says "LeBron's Mom" on the back! "I wish I could sit here and give you words to describe what my mother means to me," LeBron says. "There aren't enough words in the dictionary."

Star Gazing

The Shooting Stars played games all over the country. The competition was tough, but the team rarely lost. LeBron was the star of the Shooting Stars. By the eighth grade, he stood 6 feet tall. LeBron could do it all on the basketball court. Everyone who watched him was amazed. They wondered how someone so young could be so talented.

Fast Fact

In his first year of peewee football, LeBron scored 19 touchdowns.

LeBron had not even started high school, and he was already famous. His legend was beginning to grow.

CHAPTER 3

Mr. Basketball

As the fall of 1999 neared, LeBron had to decide where he would go to high school. Coaches all over Ohio waited nervously. LeBron's three best friends from the Shooting Stars would join him. They called themselves "the Fab Four." They would turn their new school into a **powerhouse**.

The Fab Four chose Saint Vincent-Saint Mary High School in Akron. It was one of the best schools in the state. The Fighting Irish also had a **tradition** of success in basketball.

The Fab Four (from left): LeBron James, Sian Cotton, Willie McGee, and Dru Joyce III

On the Rise

LeBron made the **varsity** basketball team as a freshman. In his first year of high school, he became the team's leader. The Irish went 27–0 and won the state championship.

The team looked up to LeBron as he began his sophomore season. He had grown 4 inches over the summer! He now stood 6 foot 7 inches and weighed more than 200 pounds.

Fast Fact

LeBron's cousin Maverick Carter was the top player for the Fighting Irish when LeBron joined the team.

Football Hero

Basketball wasn't LeBron's only sport in high school. He was also a talented receiver on the Fighting Irish football team. Some believe that LeBron could have played in the National Football League. As a sophomore, he was voted All-State. As a junior, he helped Saint Vincent-Saint Mary reach the state semifinals. LeBron gave up football to focus on basketball in his senior year.

Fast Fact

LeBron was a good student in high school. He had a B average in most of his classes. His favorite class was Earth science.

Drawing Crowds

Even after his growth spurt, LeBron was still the quickest player on the court. Basketball fans all over the state knew about him. They crammed into arenas to watch him play. The Fighting Irish had to move their home games to college arenas to hold the huge crowds. College coaches and NBA **scouts** were usually in the stands. They wanted to find out whether LeBron was the real deal. He rarely let them down.

Rising Star

LeBron led Saint Vincent-Saint Mary to the state championship for the second year in a row. After the season, he was named Ohio's "Mr. Basketball." He was the first sophomore in state history to win the award.

LeBron was becoming a national sensation. His idol, Michael Jordan, invited him to a workout with NBA players. Magazines and newspapers wrote stories about LeBron. Nike and Adidas, two of the biggest sneaker companies in the world, hoped to sign him to an advertising contract.

Fast Fact

LeBron's hero is NBA legend Michael Jordan. LeBron wears number 23 in Jordan's honor.

Under Pressure

As LeBron's fame grew, so did the pressure on him. It seemed that everyone was watching his every move. Everything he did was front-page news. *Sports Illustrated* even put him on its cover!

Through it all, LeBron kept a level head. He worked on his speech problem and learned to overcome it. Family and friends helped him stay on track, too. "I've got my friends to keep me cool," he said. "As long as you've got friends, you've got nothing to worry about."

LeBron shakes hands with future NBA star Carmelo Anthony (right). LeBron played against some of the country's top high school players.

All Eyes on the King

Saint Vincent-Saint Mary played a tough schedule during LeBron's junior season. Schools all over the country wanted a chance to beat the best. The pressure on LeBron increased, but he only seemed to get better. Again, he was named Ohio's Mr. Basketball. He was also named the national high school player of the year in 2002.

Senior Moments

Nothing could compare to the attention focused on LeBron during his senior year. Many of his games were broadcast on national television. Announcer Bill Walton was in awe. "I believe LeBron James would start on any NBA team today," he said.

With all eyes on him, LeBron enjoyed another fantastic season. He was again voted Mr. Basketball and player of the year. He also led the Fighting Irish to their third state title in four years. After the season, one question was on everyone's mind: Would LeBron play college basketball or jump straight to the NBA?

LeBron drives to the hoop during his senior season at Saint Vincent-Saint Mary.

Going Pro

What does it feel like to have the eyes of the entire basketball world on you? LeBron found out during the spring of 2003. On April 25, he announced that he was skipping college and entering the **NBA Draft**. The news created a buzz from coast to coast. Every NBA team hoped for the chance to pick him. Only one would win the "LeBron Lottery."

The Cleveland Cavaliers were one of the worst teams in the NBA. They had won only 17 games during the 2002–03 season. The Cavs ended up with the first pick in the draft. As expected, they took LeBron.

LeBron is all smiles after being picked by the Cavaliers in the 2003 NBA Draft.

Staying Home

LeBron couldn't have been happier. He had rooted for the Cavs as a kid. In addition, Cleveland was an easy drive from Akron, so LeBron's family and friends would be nearby. He also believed that he would lead the Cavs to the top of the NBA. "This is a longtime dream," LeBron said.

Fast Fact

Nike was very confident that LeBron would be a star. The company signed him to a $90 million contract before he played his first NBA game.

Age Limit

The NBA Draft was originally meant only for college players. By the late 1990s, however, NBA teams were picking high school stars every year. Kevin Garnett, Kobe Bryant, and LeBron were drafted out of high school. In 2006, the league changed its rules. It placed an age limit on players who could be drafted. As a result, NBA teams are no longer allowed to draft high schoolers.

Red-Hot Rookie

LeBron was a **rookie** for the 2003–04 season. Yet he played with the confidence of someone who had been in the NBA for many years. He led the Cavaliers in scoring, **assists**, and steals. Even more important, LeBron made his teammates better. Cleveland improved from 17 wins to 35. For his efforts, LeBron was voted NBA Rookie of the Year.

Summer Fun

That summer, LeBron joined the U.S. basketball team for the Olympics in Athens, Greece. At 19, he was the team's youngest player. Fans expected the Americans to win the gold medal. LeBron and his teammates were disappointed when they came home with the bronze.

Feeling the Heat

The 2004–05 season had its ups and downs for LeBron. He was an **All-Star** for the first time, but the Cavs didn't make the playoffs. LeBron didn't always get along with his coach, Paul Silas. When Silas was fired in 2005, many people blamed LeBron. He was criticized by fans and reporters. LeBron became even more determined to lead his team to a championship.

Fast Fact

On March 20, 2005, LeBron became the youngest player to score at least 50 points in a game. He scored 56 points against the Toronto Raptors.

Family Man

In October 2004, LeBron's life changed in a big way. His girlfriend, Savannah Brinson, gave birth to a son, LeBron Jr. (right). Their second son, Bryce, was born in 2007.

For LeBron, being a good dad means everything. He learned that lesson after growing up without knowing his own father. LeBron's kids are a reminder of the important things in life. "Being a parent, I go home and see my sons, and I forget about any mistake I ever made or the reason I'm upset," he says.

CHAPTER 5

Chasing the Dream

As the 2005–06 season opened, LeBron was focused on taking the Cavs to the playoffs. He did whatever was needed for his team to win. For the season, LeBron averaged more than 30 points a game. He was the youngest player ever to reach that level.

Thanks to LeBron, the Cavaliers rose in the **standings**. Cleveland finished second in the Central Division. The team reached the playoffs for the first time in eight years.

LeBron makes a move to the basket during his first career playoff game.

No Fear

LeBron had achieved an important goal. His next challenge was to perform under the pressure of the playoffs. "I'm not afraid," he said. "I love being here."

His confidence showed in Game 1 against the Washington Wizards. In Cleveland's 97–86 victory, LeBron recorded a **triple-double**. He had 32 points, 11 rebounds, and 11 assists.

Fast Fact

LeBron has been named Most Valuable Player of the All-Star Game twice, in 2006 and 2008.

> **"**Nothing he does surprises me anymore.**"**
>
> —Teammate Zydrunas Ilgauskas, after Game 1 of the 2006 playoffs

Buzzer Beater

In Game 3, LeBron poured in 41 points and hit the game-winning shot in the final seconds. He topped that total with 45 points in Game 5. Two nights later, Cleveland closed out the series. LeBron again made the game-winning shot.

The Cavs faced the Detroit Pistons in the next round. It was an exciting series, but Cleveland lost in seven games. Still, the Cavaliers and their fans had enjoyed a great season.

Clear Focus

LeBron had another fantastic year in 2006–07. So did the Cavs. They reached the playoffs again. LeBron was ready for a long playoff run. "I think we can win it all," he said. "That's what's on my mind right now."

Fast Fact

LeBron is good friends with rapper Jay-Z. They met when LeBron was in high school and became closer after he joined the Cavaliers. Jay-Z has even mentioned LeBron in his music.

Helping Hands

LeBron is a great leader on the court. The same is true away from it. He once treated 800 families to Thanksgiving dinner. He also donated $200,000 to victims of Hurricane Katrina and Hurricane Rita. In Akron, he hosts his annual "King for Kids" Bike-a-Thon. The event helps local charities and LeBron's Family Foundation. "I told myself if I ever made it to the level I want to be at, I'm going to give back," he says.

LeBron and Dwyane Wade (right)

Beast of the East

The Cavs opened the playoffs with a rematch against the Wizards. This time, Cleveland swept Washington in four games. Led by LeBron, the Cavs then beat the New Jersey Nets in five games. They moved on to face the Pistons in the Eastern Conference Finals.

That was the series in which LeBron took over Game 5. After closing out Game 6, the Cavs were going to the NBA Finals for the first time ever.

Fast Fact

Every June, LeBron hosts a basketball camp in Akron for boys and girls. It's known as King's Academy.

Eyes on the Prize

Unfortunately, the dream ended against the San Antonio Spurs. The Cavs lost the series in four games. LeBron and the Cavaliers returned to the playoffs in the 2007–08 season. They faced the mighty Boston Celtics in the second round and lost in seven games.

Fast Fact

LeBron was the top scorer in the NBA for the 2007–08 season. He averaged 30 points per game.

Going for the Gold

LeBron bounced back quickly from Cleveland's loss in the playoffs. Just two months later, he traveled with the U.S. basketball team to Beijing, China, for the 2008 Olympics. LeBron's last trip to the Olympics had ended in disappointment. The U.S. team had been favored to win but finished in third place.

Host With the Most

Off the court, LeBron is a big kid at heart. He loves to make people laugh. In 2006, he got to show off his skills as a comedian in television commercials for Nike. LeBron played four different characters, including one who looked like his grandfather! He hosted the comedy show *Saturday Night Live* in September 2007 and also hosted the 2007 ESPY Awards.

Find Out More

Books

Hareas, John. *Basketball*. New York: DK Children, 2005.

Stewart, Mark. *Basketball*. The Ultimate 10. Pleasantville, N.Y.: Gareth Stevens, 2009.

Stewart, Mark. *The Cleveland Cavaliers*. Team Spirit. Chicago: Norwood House, 2009.

Web Sites

NBA: LeBron James
www.nba.com/playerfile/lebron_james

U.S.A. Basketball
www.usabasketball.com

Source Notes

pp. 6, 21, 24 (top), ...
  Windhorst, Brian. ...
    ... Bron James." *Stud*... ...
    ...

    e ...
      ... Cleveland
        ...3.

.1, 25: "What's Hot." Oprah.com.
  ...tember 22, 2005. www.oprah.com/
  s... .../...ohshow/oprahshow1_
  ss_2... ...922/7

p. 15: Wahl, Grant. "On Our Radar: LeBron James, NBA-Ready." *Sports Illustrated for Kids*. June 2002.

p. 17: Wahl, Grant. "The Continuing Education of LeBron James." *Sports Illustrated*. January 11, 2003.

p. 19: "High School Basketball Phenom LeBron James Launches New Era in the NBA." *Jet*. July 14, 2003.

p. 2... "...Bron James Interview." Ins...Hoops.com. January 4, 2004. www...sidehoops.com/lebron-james-interview-010403.shtml

p. 24 (bottom): Windhorst, Brian. "Cavs Hope Stability Will Translate Into Championship." espn.com. October 16, 2006. sports.espn.go.com/nba/trainingcamp06/columns/story?id=2627814

p. 27: "USA 118, Spain 107." USABasketball.com. August 24, 2008. www.usabasketball.com/news.php?news_page=08_moly_08_quotes

Publisher's note to educators and parents: Our editors have carefully reviewed these web sites to ensure that they are suitable for children. Many web sites change frequently, however, and we cannot guarantee that a site's future contents will continue to meet our high standards of quality and educational value. Be advised that children should be closely supervised whenever they access the Internet.

Index

About the Author

Mike Kennedy is a huge sports fan who has written dozens of books for kids. He grew up in New Jersey rooting for New York teams, including the Knicks. Mike went to Franklin & Marshall College, where he earned letters in football and baseball. Today, Mike loves to run and play golf. He and his wife, Ali, live in Boulder, Colorado.